50 Hidden Kitchen Dishes for Home

By: Kelly Johnson

Table of Contents

- Secret Spice Cabinet Chicken Roast
- Hidden Herb Garden Pasta
- Underground Root Vegetable Gratin
- Forgotten Pantry Lentil Stew
- Mysterious Midnight Chocolate Cake
- Sealed Envelope Dumplings
- Tucked-Away Tandoori Shrimp
- Buried Treasure Truffle Risotto
- Lost Recipe Heirloom Tomato Soup
- Undercover Cinnamon Apple Tart
- Secret Stash Maple Glazed Salmon
- Behind-the-Door Braised Short Ribs
- Hushed Honey-Glazed Carrots
- Camouflaged Coconut Curry
- Silent Cellar Sourdough Bread
- Hidden Bay Leaf Beef Stew
- Vanishing Vanilla Bean Pudding
- Whispered Whiskey Barbecue Chicken
- Veiled Vegetable Biryani
- Under-the-Counter Clove-Spiced Cider
- Hiding-in-Plain-Sight Herb Butter Lobster
- Concealed Citrus-Marinated Pork Chops
- Secret Garden Basil Pesto Pasta
- Forgotten Spice Rack Spaghetti Sauce
- Covered-up Cranberry Brie Bites
- Disguised Dill Pickle Soup
- Locked-Away Lemon Butter Chicken
- Shrouded in Garlic Shrimp Scampi
- Hidden Hint of Nutmeg Eggnog
- Mystery Box Moroccan Tagine
- Sheltered Shakshuka with Feta
- Covert Cardamom Chai Latte
- Vaulted Vanilla & Lavender Shortbread
- Secret Ingredient Szechuan Noodles
- Behind-the-Scenes Butter Chicken

- Tightly-Sealed Teriyaki Tofu
- Undercover Olive Tapenade Toasts
- Vaulted Vinegar-Braised Cabbage
- Masquerading Maple-Bacon Brussels Sprouts
- Masked Mango-Chili Sorbet
- Unveiled Umami Mushroom Risotto
- Stealthy Star Anise Duck Breast
- Mystic Mediterranean Hummus Platter
- Shadowed Saffron Seafood Paella
- Unseen Ube Cheesecake
- Top-Secret Truffle Butter Gnocchi
- Concealed Cumin & Coriander Lamb Chops
- Buried Bourbon Brown Sugar Glaze
- Sealed Away Sesame Crusted Tuna
- Hidden Pantry Pear & Ginger Crumble

Secret Spice Cabinet Chicken Roast

Ingredients:

- 1 whole chicken
- 2 tbsp butter, softened
- 1 tsp smoked paprika
- 1/2 tsp ground cinnamon
- 1/2 tsp cumin
- 1/2 tsp coriander
- 1/4 tsp clove
- 4 cloves garlic, minced
- 1 lemon, sliced

Instructions:

1. Preheat oven to 375°F (190°C).
2. Mix butter with all the spices.
3. Rub the spice butter under the chicken skin and all over.
4. Stuff with garlic and lemon slices.
5. Roast for 1.5 hours, basting occasionally.

Hidden Herb Garden Pasta

Ingredients:

- 12 oz pasta (linguine or tagliatelle)
- 1/4 cup olive oil
- 2 cloves garlic, minced
- 1/4 cup chopped basil
- 2 tbsp chopped mint
- 2 tbsp chopped parsley
- 1/2 tsp red pepper flakes
- 1/2 cup grated Parmesan

Instructions:

1. Cook pasta and reserve 1/2 cup pasta water.
2. Sauté garlic in olive oil.
3. Toss in herbs and red pepper flakes.
4. Add pasta and reserved water, stirring well.
5. Top with Parmesan and serve.

Underground Root Vegetable Gratin

Ingredients:

- 2 potatoes, thinly sliced
- 1 sweet potato, thinly sliced
- 1 parsnip, thinly sliced
- 1 turnip, thinly sliced
- 1 cup heavy cream
- 1/2 cup Gruyère cheese, shredded
- 1/2 cup Parmesan cheese
- 1 tsp thyme
- Salt & pepper

Instructions:

1. Preheat oven to 375°F (190°C).
2. Layer root vegetables in a greased baking dish.
3. Pour cream over the top and season.
4. Sprinkle cheeses and thyme.
5. Bake for 45 minutes.

Forgotten Pantry Lentil Stew

Ingredients:

- 1 cup lentils
- 1 onion, diced
- 2 carrots, diced
- 3 cloves garlic, minced
- 1 tsp cumin
- 1/2 tsp smoked paprika
- 1/2 tsp turmeric
- 4 cups vegetable broth
- 1 can diced tomatoes

Instructions:

1. Sauté onion, carrots, and garlic.
2. Add spices and stir for 1 minute.
3. Pour in lentils, broth, and tomatoes.
4. Simmer for 30 minutes.

Mysterious Midnight Chocolate Cake

Ingredients:

- 1 1/2 cups flour
- 1 cup sugar
- 3/4 cup cocoa powder
- 1 tsp cinnamon
- 1/2 tsp cayenne pepper
- 1 tsp baking soda
- 1 cup buttermilk
- 1/2 cup vegetable oil
- 2 eggs

Instructions:

1. Preheat oven to 350°F (175°C).
2. Mix dry ingredients.
3. Whisk in buttermilk, oil, and eggs.
4. Pour into a cake pan and bake for 30 minutes.

Sealed Envelope Dumplings

Ingredients:

- 2 cups flour
- 3/4 cup water
- 1/2 lb ground pork or chicken
- 2 tbsp soy sauce
- 1 tsp ginger, minced
- 2 scallions, chopped

Instructions:

1. Mix flour and water to form dough, then rest for 30 minutes.
2. Combine filling ingredients.
3. Roll out dough, cut into circles, and fill.
4. Fold and seal edges.
5. Steam for 10 minutes.

Tucked-Away Tandoori Shrimp

Ingredients:

- 1 lb shrimp, peeled
- 1/2 cup yogurt
- 1 tbsp lemon juice
- 1 tsp cumin
- 1 tsp coriander
- 1/2 tsp turmeric
- 1/2 tsp paprika
- 1/2 tsp chili powder

Instructions:

1. Marinate shrimp for 30 minutes.
2. Grill or pan-sear until cooked.

Buried Treasure Truffle Risotto

Ingredients:

- 1 cup Arborio rice
- 3 cups chicken or vegetable broth
- 1/2 cup white wine
- 1/2 onion, diced
- 1/4 cup Parmesan cheese
- 1 tsp truffle oil

Instructions:

1. Sauté onion, add rice, and toast.
2. Deglaze with wine, then add broth gradually.
3. Stir until creamy.
4. Mix in cheese and truffle oil.

Lost Recipe Heirloom Tomato Soup

Ingredients:

- 4 heirloom tomatoes, chopped
- 1 onion, diced
- 2 cloves garlic, minced
- 2 cups vegetable broth
- 1/2 tsp thyme

Instructions:

1. Sauté onion and garlic.
2. Add tomatoes, broth, and thyme.
3. Simmer for 20 minutes, then blend.

Undercover Cinnamon Apple Tart

Ingredients:

- 1 pie crust
- 4 apples, sliced
- 1/2 cup sugar
- 1 tsp cinnamon
- 1/4 tsp nutmeg

Instructions:

1. Preheat oven to 375°F (190°C).
2. Toss apples with sugar, cinnamon, and nutmeg.
3. Arrange in crust and bake for 40 minutes.

Secret Stash Maple Glazed Salmon

Ingredients:

- 4 salmon fillets
- 1/4 cup maple syrup
- 2 tbsp soy sauce
- 1 tsp Dijon mustard
- 1 clove garlic, minced
- 1/2 tsp black pepper

Instructions:

1. Preheat oven to 400°F (200°C).
2. Mix maple syrup, soy sauce, mustard, garlic, and pepper.
3. Brush over salmon and bake for 12-15 minutes.

Behind-the-Door Braised Short Ribs

Ingredients:

- 3 lbs beef short ribs
- 2 tbsp olive oil
- 1 onion, chopped
- 3 cloves garlic, minced
- 1 cup red wine
- 2 cups beef broth
- 2 sprigs thyme
- 1 bay leaf

Instructions:

1. Sear ribs in oil, remove.
2. Sauté onion and garlic.
3. Add wine, broth, thyme, and bay leaf.
4. Return ribs, cover, and braise at 325°F (160°C) for 3 hours.

Hushed Honey-Glazed Carrots

Ingredients:

- 1 lb carrots, sliced
- 2 tbsp butter
- 2 tbsp honey
- 1/2 tsp cinnamon
- Salt & pepper

Instructions:

1. Melt butter, add honey and cinnamon.
2. Toss in carrots and cook until tender.

Camouflaged Coconut Curry

Ingredients:

- 1 lb chicken or tofu
- 1 can coconut milk
- 1 onion, diced
- 3 cloves garlic, minced
- 1 tbsp curry powder
- 1/2 tsp turmeric
- 1/2 tsp cinnamon
- 1/2 tsp ginger
- 1 tbsp lime juice

Instructions:

1. Sauté onion and garlic.
2. Add spices, chicken/tofu, and coconut milk.
3. Simmer for 20 minutes, finish with lime juice.

Silent Cellar Sourdough Bread

Ingredients:

- 500g bread flour
- 100g sourdough starter
- 325g water
- 10g salt

Instructions:

1. Mix flour, starter, and water. Rest for 30 minutes.
2. Add salt, knead, and proof overnight.
3. Shape and bake at 450°F (230°C) for 35 minutes.

Hidden Bay Leaf Beef Stew

Ingredients:

- 2 lbs beef chuck, cubed
- 2 tbsp flour
- 2 tbsp olive oil
- 1 onion, chopped
- 2 carrots, diced
- 3 bay leaves
- 1 tsp thyme
- 4 cups beef broth

Instructions:

1. Dredge beef in flour and sear.
2. Sauté onions and carrots.
3. Add broth, bay leaves, thyme, and beef.
4. Simmer for 2 hours.

Vanishing Vanilla Bean Pudding

Ingredients:

- 2 cups milk
- 1/2 cup sugar
- 1 vanilla bean, scraped
- 3 tbsp cornstarch
- 2 egg yolks

Instructions:

1. Heat milk, sugar, and vanilla.
2. Whisk cornstarch and egg yolks, temper with warm milk.
3. Return to heat and stir until thickened.

Whispered Whiskey Barbecue Chicken

Ingredients:

- 4 chicken thighs
- 1/2 cup barbecue sauce
- 2 tbsp whiskey
- 1 tbsp honey
- 1 tsp smoked paprika

Instructions:

1. Mix sauce ingredients.
2. Marinate chicken for 1 hour.
3. Grill or bake at 375°F (190°C) for 35 minutes.

Veiled Vegetable Biryani

Ingredients:

- 1 cup basmati rice
- 1 onion, sliced
- 2 cloves garlic, minced
- 1 tsp cumin
- 1/2 tsp cinnamon
- 1/2 tsp turmeric
- 2 cups mixed vegetables
- 2 cups vegetable broth

Instructions:

1. Sauté onion and garlic with spices.
2. Add rice, vegetables, and broth.
3. Cover and cook for 15 minutes.

Under-the-Counter Clove-Spiced Cider

Ingredients:

- 4 cups apple cider
- 3 cloves
- 1 cinnamon stick
- 1 star anise
- 1 orange, sliced

Instructions:

1. Simmer all ingredients for 15 minutes.
2. Strain and serve warm.

Hiding-in-Plain-Sight Herb Butter Lobster

Ingredients:

- 2 lobster tails, split in half
- 4 tbsp butter
- 2 cloves garlic, minced
- 1 tbsp parsley, chopped
- 1/2 tsp thyme
- 1/2 tsp lemon zest
- Salt & pepper

Instructions:

1. Melt butter, add garlic, parsley, thyme, and lemon zest.
2. Brush over lobster and broil for 5-7 minutes.

Concealed Citrus-Marinated Pork Chops

Ingredients:

- 4 pork chops
- 1/4 cup orange juice
- 2 tbsp lime juice
- 2 tbsp olive oil
- 2 cloves garlic, minced
- 1 tsp honey
- 1/2 tsp smoked paprika

Instructions:

1. Mix marinade and coat pork chops.
2. Marinate for 1 hour, then grill or pan-fry for 5-6 minutes per side.

Secret Garden Basil Pesto Pasta

Ingredients:

- 12 oz pasta
- 2 cups fresh basil
- 1/2 cup spinach (for a hidden boost)
- 1/3 cup pine nuts
- 2 cloves garlic
- 1/2 cup Parmesan cheese
- 1/2 cup olive oil
- Salt & pepper

Instructions:

1. Blend all ingredients except pasta.
2. Toss with cooked pasta and serve.

Forgotten Spice Rack Spaghetti Sauce

Ingredients:

- 1 can crushed tomatoes
- 1/2 onion, diced
- 3 cloves garlic, minced
- 1 tsp oregano
- 1/2 tsp cinnamon (secret ingredient!)
- 1/2 tsp nutmeg
- 1/2 tsp smoked paprika
- 1 tbsp olive oil

Instructions:

1. Sauté onions and garlic.
2. Add spices and tomatoes, simmer for 20 minutes.

Covered-up Cranberry Brie Bites

Ingredients:

- 1 sheet puff pastry
- 1 wheel brie, cut into cubes
- 1/4 cup cranberry sauce
- 1 egg, beaten

Instructions:

1. Cut pastry into squares.
2. Add brie and cranberry, fold over, and brush with egg.
3. Bake at 375°F (190°C) for 15 minutes.

Disguised Dill Pickle Soup

Ingredients:

- 4 cups chicken broth
- 3 potatoes, diced
- 1/2 cup chopped dill pickles
- 1/2 cup pickle juice
- 1/2 cup heavy cream
- 1 tbsp butter
- 1 tsp dried dill
- Salt & pepper

Instructions:

1. Cook potatoes in broth until tender.
2. Add pickles, juice, and seasonings.
3. Stir in cream and serve.

Locked-Away Lemon Butter Chicken

Ingredients:

- 4 chicken breasts
- 4 tbsp butter
- 2 cloves garlic, minced
- 1 lemon, juiced
- 1/2 tsp thyme
- Salt & pepper

Instructions:

1. Melt butter, sauté garlic, then add lemon juice and thyme.
2. Sear chicken in sauce for 6-7 minutes per side.

Shrouded in Garlic Shrimp Scampi

Ingredients:

- 12 oz shrimp, peeled
- 4 tbsp butter
- 3 cloves garlic, minced
- 1/2 cup white wine
- 1/2 tsp red pepper flakes
- 1/2 tsp lemon zest

Instructions:

1. Melt butter, sauté garlic, then add shrimp.
2. Pour in wine and seasonings, cook for 3-4 minutes.

Hidden Hint of Nutmeg Eggnog

Ingredients:

- 2 cups whole milk
- 1/2 cup heavy cream
- 3 egg yolks
- 1/4 cup sugar
- 1/2 tsp nutmeg
- 1/2 tsp vanilla

Instructions:

1. Heat milk and cream.
2. Whisk egg yolks with sugar, temper with warm milk.
3. Return to heat and cook until thickened.

Mystery Box Moroccan Tagine

Ingredients:

- 1 lb lamb or chicken, cubed
- 1 onion, chopped
- 3 cloves garlic, minced
- 1 tsp cinnamon
- 1/2 tsp cumin
- 1/2 tsp coriander
- 1/4 tsp cayenne
- 1 can diced tomatoes
- 1/4 cup dried apricots, chopped

Instructions:

1. Sear meat, then add onion and garlic.
2. Stir in spices, tomatoes, and apricots.
3. Simmer for 45 minutes.

Sheltered Shakshuka with Feta

Ingredients:

- 1 tbsp olive oil
- 1 small onion, diced
- 2 cloves garlic, minced
- 1 tsp cumin
- 1/2 tsp smoked paprika
- 1/2 tsp chili flakes
- 1 can crushed tomatoes
- 4 eggs
- 1/4 cup feta cheese, crumbled
- Salt & pepper
- Fresh cilantro, for garnish

Instructions:

1. Heat oil, sauté onion and garlic.
2. Add spices and tomatoes, simmer for 10 minutes.
3. Make wells in the sauce and crack in eggs.
4. Cover and cook until eggs are set, then sprinkle with feta and cilantro.

Covert Cardamom Chai Latte

Ingredients:

- 2 cups milk (or oat milk)
- 1 cup water
- 2 black tea bags
- 1 tsp cardamom
- 1/2 tsp cinnamon
- 1/4 tsp cloves
- 1/4 tsp nutmeg
- 1 tbsp honey or maple syrup

Instructions:

1. Heat water, add spices and tea bags, steep for 5 minutes.
2. Heat milk separately, then froth or whisk.
3. Mix with tea, sweeten, and serve warm.

Vaulted Vanilla & Lavender Shortbread

Ingredients:

- 1 cup butter, softened
- 1/2 cup sugar
- 2 cups flour
- 1/2 tsp vanilla extract
- 1/2 tsp dried lavender

Instructions:

1. Cream butter and sugar.
2. Add flour, vanilla, and lavender, mix until combined.
3. Roll and cut into shapes, then bake at 325°F (165°C) for 12-15 minutes.

Secret Ingredient Szechuan Noodles

Ingredients:

- 8 oz noodles
- 2 tbsp soy sauce
- 1 tbsp Szechuan chili oil
- 1 tbsp rice vinegar
- 1 tsp honey
- 1 tbsp peanut butter (secret ingredient!)
- 2 cloves garlic, minced
- 1/2 tsp ginger, grated
- Green onions and sesame seeds for garnish

Instructions:

1. Cook noodles, reserve 1/4 cup cooking water.
2. Mix all sauce ingredients, add water to thin.
3. Toss with noodles and garnish.

Behind-the-Scenes Butter Chicken

Ingredients:

- 2 chicken breasts, cubed
- 1/2 cup yogurt
- 1 tbsp garam masala
- 1 tbsp butter
- 1 onion, chopped
- 2 cloves garlic, minced
- 1 tbsp ginger
- 1 can tomato puree
- 1/2 cup heavy cream

Instructions:

1. Marinate chicken in yogurt and spices for 30 minutes.
2. Cook onion, garlic, and ginger in butter.
3. Add chicken, then tomato puree.
4. Simmer, then stir in cream before serving.

Tightly-Sealed Teriyaki Tofu

Ingredients:

- 1 block firm tofu, cubed
- 2 tbsp soy sauce
- 1 tbsp honey
- 1 tsp sesame oil
- 1 tsp ginger, grated
- 1 clove garlic, minced
- 1 tbsp cornstarch

Instructions:

1. Toss tofu in cornstarch, pan-fry until golden.
2. Mix sauce ingredients, pour over tofu, and cook until thickened.

Undercover Olive Tapenade Toasts

Ingredients:

- 1/2 cup black olives
- 1/2 cup green olives
- 1 tbsp capers
- 1 clove garlic
- 1 tbsp lemon juice
- 2 tbsp olive oil
- Baguette slices

Instructions:

1. Blend all ingredients except bread.
2. Spread on toasted baguette slices.

Vaulted Vinegar-Braised Cabbage

Ingredients:

- 1/2 head red cabbage, shredded
- 2 tbsp apple cider vinegar
- 1 tbsp brown sugar
- 1 tsp mustard seeds
- 1 tbsp butter
- Salt & pepper

Instructions:

1. Sauté cabbage in butter.
2. Add vinegar, sugar, and mustard seeds, simmer until soft.

Masquerading Maple-Bacon Brussels Sprouts

Ingredients:

- 1 lb Brussels sprouts, halved
- 4 strips bacon, chopped
- 2 tbsp maple syrup
- 1 tbsp balsamic vinegar

Instructions:

1. Cook bacon, then remove and use drippings to fry Brussels sprouts.
2. Add maple syrup and vinegar, toss, and return bacon before serving.

Masked Mango-Chili Sorbet

Ingredients:

- 2 cups mango, cubed
- 1/4 cup lime juice
- 1 tbsp honey
- 1/4 tsp chili powder

Instructions:

1. Blend all ingredients.
2. Freeze for 3 hours, stirring occasionally.

Unveiled Umami Mushroom Risotto

Ingredients:

- 1 cup arborio rice
- 4 cups vegetable broth
- 1/2 cup white wine
- 1 cup mushrooms, sliced
- 1 onion, diced
- 2 cloves garlic, minced
- 1/4 cup Parmesan
- 1 tsp miso paste (secret ingredient!)

Instructions:

1. Sauté onion, garlic, and mushrooms.
2. Add rice, then deglaze with wine.
3. Slowly add broth, stirring, until absorbed.
4. Stir in Parmesan and miso before serving.

Stealthy Star Anise Duck Breast

Ingredients:

- 2 duck breasts
- 2 star anise pods
- 1 tbsp soy sauce
- 1 tbsp honey
- 1 tsp five-spice powder
- 1/2 tsp black pepper
- 1 clove garlic, minced

Instructions:

1. Score the duck skin, season with five-spice and pepper.
2. Cook skin-side down in a cold pan over medium heat until crispy, then flip and cook 3-4 minutes more.
3. Remove duck and add garlic, star anise, soy sauce, and honey to the pan. Simmer until thick.
4. Slice duck and drizzle with sauce before serving.

Mystic Mediterranean Hummus Platter

Ingredients:

- 1 can chickpeas, drained
- 2 tbsp tahini
- 2 tbsp olive oil
- 1 clove garlic
- 1 tbsp lemon juice
- 1/2 tsp cumin
- 1/4 tsp smoked paprika
- 1 tbsp chopped parsley
- Pita, olives, cucumbers, and roasted peppers for serving

Instructions:

1. Blend all ingredients until smooth.
2. Spread on a plate, drizzle with olive oil, and sprinkle with extra paprika and parsley.
3. Serve with pita and toppings.

Shadowed Saffron Seafood Paella

Ingredients:

- 1 cup Arborio rice
- 1/2 tsp saffron threads, soaked in 2 tbsp warm water
- 2 cups seafood stock
- 1/2 cup white wine
- 1/2 lb shrimp
- 1/2 lb mussels
- 1 onion, chopped
- 2 cloves garlic, minced
- 1 tsp smoked paprika
- 1 tomato, diced

Instructions:

1. Sauté onion, garlic, and tomato in olive oil.
2. Stir in rice and saffron water, then add wine and stock.
3. Simmer until rice is tender, then add seafood and cook until done.

Unseen Ube Cheesecake

Ingredients:

- 1 1/2 cups crushed graham crackers
- 1/4 cup butter, melted
- 2 cups cream cheese
- 1 cup ube halaya (purple yam jam)
- 1/2 cup sugar
- 2 eggs
- 1/2 cup heavy cream
- 1 tsp vanilla

Instructions:

1. Mix graham crackers with butter, press into a springform pan.
2. Blend cream cheese, ube, sugar, eggs, and vanilla until smooth.
3. Pour over the crust and bake at 325°F (165°C) for 50 minutes.

Top-Secret Truffle Butter Gnocchi

Ingredients:

- 1 lb potato gnocchi
- 2 tbsp butter
- 1 tsp truffle oil
- 1/4 cup Parmesan
- 1 clove garlic, minced
- 1 tbsp chopped parsley

Instructions:

1. Cook gnocchi in salted boiling water until they float.
2. Sauté garlic in butter, then toss in gnocchi and truffle oil.
3. Sprinkle with Parmesan and parsley before serving.

Concealed Cumin & Coriander Lamb Chops

Ingredients:

- 4 lamb chops
- 1 tsp ground cumin
- 1 tsp ground coriander
- 1 clove garlic, minced
- 1 tbsp olive oil
- 1/2 tsp salt

Instructions:

1. Rub lamb chops with oil, spices, and garlic.
2. Sear in a hot pan for 3-4 minutes per side.
3. Let rest before serving.

Buried Bourbon Brown Sugar Glaze

Ingredients:

- 1/2 cup bourbon
- 1/2 cup brown sugar
- 1 tbsp Dijon mustard
- 1 tbsp apple cider vinegar
- 1/2 tsp salt

Instructions:

1. Simmer all ingredients until thickened.
2. Brush onto meats or roasted vegetables.

Sealed Away Sesame-Crusted Tuna

Ingredients:

- 2 tuna steaks
- 1/4 cup sesame seeds
- 1 tbsp soy sauce
- 1/2 tsp wasabi paste
- 1 tbsp sesame oil

Instructions:

1. Coat tuna in sesame seeds.
2. Sear in sesame oil for 1-2 minutes per side.
3. Mix soy sauce and wasabi for dipping.

Hidden Pantry Pear & Ginger Crumble

Ingredients:

- 4 pears, sliced
- 1/4 cup sugar
- 1 tsp grated ginger
- 1/2 tsp cinnamon
- 1/2 cup oats
- 1/4 cup flour
- 1/4 cup brown sugar
- 2 tbsp butter

Instructions:

1. Toss pears with sugar, ginger, and cinnamon, place in a baking dish.
2. Mix oats, flour, brown sugar, and butter until crumbly, sprinkle on top.
3. Bake at 350°F (175°C) for 30 minutes.

www.ingramcontent.com/pod-product-compliance
Lightning Source LLC
LaVergne TN
LVHW081339060526
838201LV00055B/2734